Tips for
Your Juicer

Tips for Your Juicer

JOY SKIPPER

EBURY
PRESS

3 5 7 9 10 8 6 4 2

Ebury Press, an imprint of Ebury Publishing,
20 Vauxhall Bridge Road,
London, SW1V 2SA

Ebury Press is part of the Penguin Random House group of companies whose
addresses can be found at global.penguinrandomhouse.com

Penguin
Random House
UK

First published by Ebury Press in 2008
This edition first published by Ebury Press in 2015

www.eburypublishing.co.uk

A CIP catalogue record for this book is available from the British Library

ISBN: 9781785032783

Printed and bound in Great Britain by Clays Ltd, St Ives PLC

Penguin Random House is committed to a sustainable future for our business,
our readers and our planet. This book is made from Forest Stewardship
Council® certified paper.

MIX
Paper | Supporting
responsible forestry
FSC® C018179

Contents

introduction

With your own juicer you can decide exactly what goes into your daily glass of refreshment, and therefore into your body.

You may now be the proud owner of a shiny new juicer. Is this likely to be yet another kitchen appliance that you will use to death for the first month, only to banish it to the back of the cupboard never to resurface again? Hopefully not, as there are so many great reasons for using your juicer on a regular basis: the juice has a far superior taste and nutritional value; you have control over the ingredients; you're free to experiment; by using up leftover fruit and veg, you cut down on waste; it helps you stay fit and healthy; you can help to save the planet. And on top of all that, it's fun!

Pre-packed juices and smoothies have certainly improved over the years, but if you look closely you'll still find lots of additives (mainly sweeteners) and preservatives that aren't top of the healthy-living list of must-haves. Making your own juice is not only cheaper than buying a ready-made carton, it's much healthier, too. Juicing for health has been scientifically proved, with immune-boosting combinations of vitamins that can ward off colds and flu, help to cure fevers and maintain a healthy digestive system.

Making your own drinks means you have total control over the taste, the nutrients (to a point obviously) and the cost. Taste is a very personal thing and it will take you a while to get used to your juicer, knowing how much of each fruit, handful of leaves or pinch of spice to add to each drink. But that's all part of the fun of juicing – experiment every day with different ingredients. There is only so much food you can eat, but you can certainly drink a lot more!

By helping you to understand how to get the most out of your juicer, from choosing a suitable model to preparing ingredients, this book will unleash the full potential of your new gadget, giving you some fantastic recipe ideas to get you started and some top tips on troubleshooting if things aren't going to plan. Above all, why not see this as a great opportunity to combine experimental cooking with a healthy lifestyle?

top juicing tips

- Always leave your juicer on the work surface where it can be seen – and used.

- Always soak or clean your juicer immediately after use – you will regret it if you don't!

- Buy fruit and vegetables in season – they are cheaper and tastier.

- Don't worry about what you mix together. Be brave and try unusual combinations – you may be pleasantly surprised!

- Drink your juice as soon as possible – it will lose nutrients very quickly.

healthy juicing

- **Vital Nutrients**

- **Juice Detox**

vital nutrients

Is juicing really healthy and if so, why? For the last few years health officials have been nagging us all to have at least five portions of fruit and vegetables a day, and there is a very good reason for this. Fruit and vegetables are full of vitamins, minerals, antioxidants, phytochemicals, fibre and even water – all vital to help keep our bodies fit and healthy. Freshly made juice can provide all of this in one glass.

Antioxidants help to rid our bodies of the free radicals that come from bad diet choices, lack of exercise or just the process of getting old. Choose coloured fruit and vegetables for the best antioxidants – berries are fantastic; blueberries, strawberries, raspberries and blackberries. Colourful peppers, carrots and dark green leafy vegetables will also help – try to imagine a rainbow of fruit and vegetables going into your juice and you won't be going far wrong.

Over the last few years there has been talk of 'superfoods', and how important they are in the diet. These tend to be foods that are beneficial to health in one way or another – broccoli is a great example as it is rich in so many vitamins and minerals and will help improve the skin, the immune system and the liver. Not all superfoods are fruit and vegetables: even prunes and yogurt come into this category.

five a day

Trying to eat at least five portions a day can sometimes seem a little daunting, and even cooking can reduce the nutritional benefits. The best way to get all the nutrients that fruit and veg have to offer is to eat them raw, and juicing is the perfect way of doing this. Bear in mind that two portions of fruit and vegetables only count as one when they are juiced, as you are removing the fibre, but your body will be able to absorb all the other nutrients more easily as it does not have to break them down, because the juicer has already done that for you.

fibre

The one nutrient you will not be getting through juicing is fibre – that is what is left in the pulp. Because of this it is best not to consume too many fruit juices as they are very high in sugar – the fibre would normally help the body to absorb the sugar more slowly, and without it you will get a rush of sugar into the bloodstream which in turn could increase your insulin levels. Sweeter root vegetables, such as carrots and parsnips, are also high in sugar, so watch the quantities of these that you consume.

juice detox

Our bodies are constantly being bombarded with toxins from outside influences such as pesticides, pollution or smoking, as well as the toxins our body produces through the metabolic process, for example lactic acid. The occasional detox to try and rid the body of these toxins is beneficial, and juicing your own organic fruit and vegetables can certainly help. Be aware of the low fibre content of juice, as sometimes this can cause a reabsorption of toxins into the body.

There are certain fruits and vegetables that help the liver to detox, and obviously it is important that they are organic or you will be taking in more toxins with your juice:

• Brassicas – cabbage, broccoli, Brussels sprouts

• Vitamin B-rich foods – nuts, seeds, vegetables, salads

• Vitamin C-rich foods – peppers, watercress, cabbage

• Citrus fruits – oranges, tangerines (not grapefruit)

• Fibre – apples

Note Grapefruit should be taken with caution as it can slow down part of the process of detoxification and also affect medication. Always consult a medical practitioner before embarking on a detox programme, especially if you are taking any medicines.

✔ **TIP**

Don't drink juices quickly. As with food that needs to be chewed thoroughly before swallowing, take time to savour your juice, too. Enzymes start to work on your food the minute it is in your mouth, so take your time both eating and drinking to ensure maximum nutrient intake.

before you begin

- Finding the Machine for You

- Finding a Home for Your Juicer

- Juicing Gadgets and Equipment

- Cleaning Your Juicer

- Manufacturer's Instructions

finding the machine for you

One of the most frequently asked questions is 'which machine is the best?' There are two main types of juicer: centrifugal and masticating. To help in your decision and to get the best juicer for your budget and lifestyle, consider the following questions before you buy:

• How much do you want to spend? If you are new to juicing it may be worth investing in a small, less expensive model to start with and then upgrade at a later stage. The internet is also a great place for comparing prices.

• What do you want to juice? Some juicers aren't suited to more unusual ingredients, such as wheatgrass.

• How much juice will it hold? A juicer that produces a single glass of juice each time may not suit a family.

• How easy is it to clean? Some juicers can be dismantled and put in the dishwasher.

• How much space will it take up in your kitchen? If you intend to use your juicer on a regular basis, it makes sense for it to sit on your work surface and not be hidden away in a cupboard.

- How noisy is it? Unless you try before you buy you're unlikely to find this out before you turn it on, but ask for recommendations from friends or check juicer reviews in magazines or on the internet before you buy.

centrifugal juicers

These work by shredding the fruit or vegetable with a high-speed spinning blade at the base of a basket that has fine holes in it, which sieve the juice as it is forced through and out of the spout. The pulp is either left in the basket or is spun off and collected in a separate container.

Centrifugal juicers are the fastest method of juicing, although the high revs mean that more oxygen is incorporated, which reduces the shelf life of the juice (not an issue as it is recommended that you drink fresh juices instantly) and some juices will appear 'frothy'.

One downside is the pulp left in the basket which needs to be emptied before another batch is made. Centrifugal juicers are not good at juicing greens and will not juice wheatgrass.

masticating juicers

These work by crushing or masticating fruit and vegetables with a slow turning screw or auger. They generally work at a slower pace than the centrifugal types, but do yield more juice. Generally, masticating juicers are quieter than centrifugal machines. There are several different types:

- *The Champion* – cylindrical in shape, this has stainless steel teeth across the length of the cutter, which crush or 'chew' the produce. The juice is then squeezed through a strainer or juicing screen and the pulp is extracted from a nozzle at the end. This enables you to juice continuously without having to stop and empty the pulp. Fit a collecting bag on the end or place the machine over a tray for catching the pulp. Wheatgrass cannot be juiced in this machine.

- *Single gear juicers* – these machines also use a slowly rotating screw but are similar to a mincing machine. The process is slower than that of the centrifugal or The Champion machines, but the produce is damaged less which means that oxidation takes less time, the juice stays fresher for slightly longer and the nutritional content is higher.

- *Twin gear juicers* – these are the best machines available and will juice practically anything you put in them! Fruit and vegetables are crushed between the gears and the juice is pressed out through a juicing screen, with the pulp being ejected out of the front of the machine. The machine is much slower than the centrifugal machines, but the quality of the juice is much higher and the yield certainly the highest of all. Twin gear juicers also excel at fibrous types of produce, such as all leafy greens and especially wheatgrass. Twin gear juicers are trickier to clean than most and the feeding tube is sometimes narrower, requiring more chopping before you start.

citrus juicers

A citrus juicer is designed purely for juicing citrus – oranges, grapefruit, lemons and limes. You cannot use it for any other fruit or vegetables. Some normal juicers come with a citrus juicer attachment so you can choose the way you juice your citrus fruits. You would normally get more juice with a citrus juicer than doing it by hand.

juicing features

Some twin gear juicers come with a blank screen that can be used to produce homogenised foods, nut butters and sorbets. Some models are capable of making pasta and grinding grains. You may find you have different thickness juicing screens – this will give you thicker or thinner juice.

The size of the feeding chamber may vary on different machines – this is where you feed in the chopped fruit and vegetables. If the chamber is very small it means more time taken chopping your ingredients into smaller chunks or slices.

Some machines come with separate citrus attachments that enable you to juice citrus fruits without peeling them first. Obviously if you are blending other fruit with the citrus fruits it makes sense to do them all together. You also tend to get more pulp in the juice with the citrus attachment.

Another add-on with some machines is a coulis maker, which enables you to produce thicker juices or nectars for making desserts, soups or jellies. For example, in a juicer pear juice will be clear, but the coulis maker will give a much thicker, nectar-type juice.

finding a home for your juicer

As with most kitchen appliances, if your machine is out of sight it will be out of mind – when you think about making a juice and you have to dig to the back of the cupboard to retrieve your juicer, you probably won't bother. Don't let it happen with your juicer!

Keep it out, on the work surface, in an area where it is easy to reach and hopefully it will then become an everyday habit.

Make the space around your juicer easy to work in, with everything at hand and organised, then when you sleepily wander down early in the morning to make your wake-up juice it will seem easy and effortless.

juicing gadgets and equipment

Having the essential equipment and ingredients close to hand will also make the juicing experience easy and enjoyable.

fruit bowl
Keeping some fruits in a fruit bowl by your juicer also ensures that all your ingredients are not ice-cold in your juice (sometimes in winter this

can be a little too much of a shock to the body first thing in the morning). You will also be able to see which fruits you need to replace or make a decision on which juice you will make.

chopping board

Placing the juicer on a heavy, sturdy chopping board will also ensure you can work in one place, chopping or peeling your fruit and vegetables before feeding them directly into the machine.

Fruit and vegetables only have to be chopped in order to fit them into your juicer's feeding tube – if you have a wide feeding tube then not much chopping is involved (preferable!).

If you are including leaves, e.g. spinach, watercress or herbs, it is best to add these either enclosed in other fruits or squeezed into a tight ball, and to feed other fruit or vegetables after them to ensure they all go through. Garlic is best put through the juicer first, to prevent the strong smell sticking to the machine. Other than that, there are no rules about what goes in first or last.

collecting jug

Not all machines come with a collecting jug or container, so make sure whatever you choose will fit underneath the pouring spout of the machine. A jug is a good idea when you are juicing enough for two or three people.

very sharp knife

This is one of the most important pieces of kitchen equipment. There are more accidents with blunt knives than sharp ones – putting too much pressure on a blunt knife can cause you to slip. A sharp knife needs no pressure and will slice your fruit and vegetables without any effort.

If you don't have a knife sharpener, make friends with your local butcher or fishmonger; they know the importance of sharp knives and I'm sure will be willing to help. Failing that, invest in a knife 'steel' or an electric knife sharpener: these will do a very professional job.

blenders

Use a blender rather than a food processor (although this will work too) to make the best smoothies. It is possible to buy a single blender or one that is attached to a food processor. A blender always requires liquid for it to work, so yogurt, milk or juices are always needed for your smoothies.

sprouters

For sprouting beans and seeds all you really need is a glass jar with a perforated lid to enable you to rinse and drain the contents over a few days while they sprout. Dedicated sprouters are available (check on the internet) which does make the process slightly easier as they may come with their own draining apparatus.

cleaning your juicer

Some juicing machines are easier to clean than others and some even allow parts of the machine to be put into a dishwasher, which makes life much easier. Check with the manufacturer's instructions before placing any part of the machine into a dishwasher – if in doubt, hand wash.

soaking

While you are preparing your fruit and vegetables for juicing, run a big washing-up bowl of hot soapy water. As soon as you have finished juicing, take the machine apart and scrape out as much of the pulp as possible from all the nooks and crannies (some machines come with a perfectly shaped spatula to help you do this).

Place all the difficult to clean bits of the machine, such as the juicing screen, into the hot soapy water and while you drink your delicious juice, leave them to soak. Most manufacturers recommend that you don't soak any part of the machine in detergents for too long, so never leave it for longer than it takes to drink your juice. Soaking softens the fibres slightly and makes them easier to brush or scrub off.

> ✔ **QUICK TIP**
>
> *What to do with the leftover pulp? As you need to soak or wash your machine quickly after use you will need somewhere to empty the pulp – not in the rubbish bin, it's far too good to waste! Find a small plastic container with a lid that you can keep near your machine. Empty the pulp into the container each time you use the juicer, and when it gets full it can be emptied onto your garden, or even better, your compost heap.*

scrubbing

After soaking use a washing-up brush (or nail brush) to scrub away at the bits still stuck in the mesh. Scrub in the soapy water and then under a running tap to allow the water to drain all the bits away. Rinse thoroughly.

 QUICK TIP
Twin gear juicers are probably the most difficult to clean. If you are using them more than once a day, keep the difficult to clean parts in some clean water between juicing and then clean thoroughly at the end of the day.

manufacturer's instructions

If you are new to juicing, take the time to read the hints and tips in this book and in your manufacturer's handbook before you start. Practise first with a few simple ingredients until you are familiar with the way your machine works.

basic ingredients

- Fruit

- Vegetables

- Herbs

- Spices

- Unusual Ingredients

fruit

Try and buy organic produce for all your ingredients whenever possible – or grow your own. That way you are absolutely sure what is going into your juice and therefore into your body. Even the smallest garden or window box can produce delicious strawberries or tomatoes.

Farmers' markets are a great source of unusual varieties of fruit and vegetables. Familiarise yourself with seasonal produce and try to buy local produce when in season – you'll soon notice the difference between flavours and levels of sweetness.

To prepare fruit simply wash, discard any pith or stones/pips and chop the flesh into pieces small enough to go through the feeder tube of your juicer. Most fruits do not need to be peeled (with a few exceptions), and this way you retain the nutrients that are just below the skin.

frozen or tinned fruits?

Frozen fruit is great as it enables you to use fruits that may be out of season and, as these fruits have normally been frozen when super fresh, they will have retained all their nutrients. Always defrost fruits before juicing, preferably catching the natural juices that will run out during the defrosting.

Tinned fruits are often in syrup or may have gone through a process before being tinned so it is probably best to avoid these as they could be high in sugar.

nutritional terms explained

* *Antioxidant* – a substance that helps to fight the free radicals in our bodies, protecting cells from damage.

* *Beta-carotene* – a powerful antioxidant, which the body transforms into vitamin A needed for healthy skin and protection against infections.

* *Bioflavonoids* – help vitamin C to work and act as antioxidants, mainly found in berries and citrus fruits.

* *Bromelain* – an enzyme found in pineapples which helps digestion.

* *B vitamins* – important for energy production.

* *Calcium* – mineral required by the body for clotting blood, contracting muscles and improving bone and teeth health, to name just a few.

* *Carotenoids*, such as beta-carotene – the compounds that give fruit and vegetables their colour, normally in the pigment of their skin.

* *Ellagic acid* – a compound that has been shown to prevent carcinogens from turning healthy cells into cancerous ones.

* *Fibre* – needed for a healthy digestive system and to help the removal of waste products from the body.

* *Folic acid* – a vitamin needed for brain and nerve functions, and critical during pregnancy.

* *Iron* – a component of the blood and vital for energy production.

* *Magnesium* – a mineral that helps relaxation, great for PMS and essential for energy production.

* *Oxidation* – a chemical reaction with air that leads to the deterioration of plant cells.

* *Pectin* – insoluble fibre that helps to eliminate toxins from the body, such as cholesterol.

* *Phytochemicals* – plant chemicals that are not classed as nutrients but are needed for us to remain healthy.

* *Potassium* – a mineral that enables nutrients to move into our bodies and for waste materials to move out!

basic ingredients

* *Selenium* – an antioxidant that helps to protect our bodies and also good for metabolism.

* *Vitamin C* – a vital nutrient and antioxidant, needed for a healthy immune system and for improved skin condition.

* *Vitamin E* – an antioxidant which protects our cells from damage, also very good for the skin.

Try to buy your fresh fruit and vegetables from a reputable local greengrocer who has a high turnover of supplies, therefore ensuring you are getting the freshest produce available. Always try and choose produce yourself so you know it is ripe and ready for juicing!

apples

As well as adding lots of sweetness to your juices, apples are great at helping the body to get rid of unwanted toxins, as they are rich in pectin. They also contain malic and tartaric acids, which improve the digestion and breakdown of fats, as well as an abundance of vitamin C to help boost your immune system.

Apples seem to combine happily with just about all fruit and vegetables in juicing and different varieties of apple will give different flavours and levels of sweetness.

apricots

Apricots are a rich source of beta-carotenes, which the body converts into vitamin A – important for immunity against infection, healthy skin and good eyesight, as well as helping protect against cancer. They are also rich in potassium and magnesium which helps increase energy and great for boosting iron intake. Remove the stone and chop the flesh.

bananas

Despite all the rumours, bananas are not fattening but are packed with great nutrients – potassium, iron, zinc, folic acid and calcium, as well as pectin. Always use ripe bananas as the starch in unripe ones is not easily digested.

basic ingredients

Add bananas to thicken smoothies but definitely not for juicing! Banana-based smoothies give lots of instant and slow-releasing energy.

blackberries

Rich in vitamins C and E, blackberries are a great antioxidant, which helps boost the immune system. In season, freshly picked wild blackberries tend to have a better flavour than the oversized cultivated variety found in supermarkets throughout the year.

blackcurrants

Very high in vitamin C, far higher than the same weight in oranges! The pigment in their skin also contains anthocyanosides, which are antibacterial and anti-inflammatory.

blueberries

One of the most health-protecting foods, blueberries are very rich in antioxidants. Although they can be juiced, blueberries are probably best used in a smoothie combined with other soft fruits, as they can be expensive to use in large quantities.

cherries

Rich in antioxidants, cherries also contain ellagic acid, which gives them anti-cancer properties, and are rich in folic acid, the B vitamins and vitamins C and E, together with a large number of minerals. The darker fruits have the higher nutritional content. Remove the stone from cherries before juicing.

coconut

Drinking and cooking with fresh coconut milk is an exotic experience that cannot be beaten! First, crack your coconut. Start by piercing one of the eyes with a sharp knife – these are the small dark spots at one end of the coconut. Collect the water from the coconut in a small glass. Smash the whole coconut with a hammer in the middle where it is widest, then remove the white fleshy bits. Put the flesh through the juicer then pour in the coconut water too – this will rinse away the pulp and give you coconut milk.

Buy coconuts that are heavy for their size, store in the fridge and use within one week of buying. Tinned coconut milk can be used as an alternative and for adding to smoothies.

cranberries

Cranberries contain substances that stick to the lining of the bladder, kidneys and intestinal tracts and prevent bacteria from attaching. They are renowned for the treatment of cystitis. Neat cranberry juice is quite sharp so will always taste better when mixed with a sweeter juice, such as apple. Frozen berries are now available throughout the year.

figs

Figs are well known for their laxative effect so take care when juicing them! They contain a natural chemical called ficin, which starts the breakdown of proteins in the body and improves digestion. They are also rich in potassium, iron, fibre and beta-carotene as well as an anti-cancer agent called benzaldehyde.

Figs can be expensive so make the most of them when they are in season and reasonably priced. Use the whole, unpeeled fruit.

grapefruit

Like all citrus fruits, grapefruits are very high in vitamin C – great for boosting the immune system. They are also a good source of potassium and bioflavonoids, which are important for the heart and circulation, and contain pectin, the fibre that helps eliminate cholesterol from the body and helps digestive problems. However, some medication reacts badly to grapefruit juice so do consult your doctor before drinking in large amounts.

Pink, ruby and white grapefruit have different flavours and sweetness. To obtain as many nutrients as possible, just peel the grapefruit and add to the juicer as normal – the good bits are normally in the pith!

Note Be careful when drinking grapefruit juice if on medication or trying to detox – speak to your medical practitioner first.

grapes

Grapes contain an enormous amount of antioxidants and are therefore great all-round protectors against heart and circulatory diseases as well as cancer. Red grapes are higher in antioxidants, as the nutrients are found in the colourful skin. However, grapes are naturally high in sugar. Buy grapes that are organic or have not been sprayed, and look for firm, unbruised fruit.

guava

Rich in vitamin C, the guava is a relative of cinnamon, cloves, allspice and nutmeg. It is also rich in B vitamins, fibre and calcium.

basic ingredients

kiwi fruit

Kiwi fruit contains an abundance of vitamin C and fibre, as well as potassium in large amounts, which helps prevent cramps, insomnia and depression. In the last few years the green kiwi fruit has been joined by the golden kiwi – just as tasty and nutritious.

kumquats

Sharing many characteristics with their citrus close relatives, kumquats have a very sweet outer skin and amazing tart flesh inside – they are not to be peeled, but eaten whole (without pips) so you get the benefit of both tartness and sweetness together. They are in season from December to June and are rich in potassium and vitamins A and C. Pop them in the juicer whole.

lemon

Lemon juice has been used for years as a tonic, for example hot lemon and honey to soothe a sore throat. It has great cleansing properties and helps the elimination of toxins from the body and helps prevent oxidation in freshly cut fruit, so adding some to your juice will keep it fresher just a little longer.

Lemons can be juiced with the skins on or off – leaving the skin on does make the juice a little sharp so experiment and see which you prefer.

lime

From the same family as lemons, limes are similar in nutritional content with slightly less vitamin C. Buy dark green limes as these tend to have more juice. Keep them at room temperature and roll around with the heel of the hand on a work surface to soften before juicing.

lychees

This is an unusual fruit but worth trying. Don't use tinned lychees as the flavour is inferior. Peel the tough skin and remove the stones before juicing.

mango

Apart from tasting amazing, one mango will provide you with more than a day's requirement of vitamin C as well as good amounts of vitamins A and E, fibre, potassium and iron. The juice from a mango is thick and there is not much to show after processing (compared to eating the whole fruit), but the flavour is so wonderful it is worth it! Mix it with other tropical fruits or pour it over ice.

Buy mangoes that are slightly tender when squeezed and keep them at room temperature so they continue to ripen.

melons

There are many types of melon but, for maximum nutritional benefits, watermelon and cantaloupe are the best. They are great for cleansing the kidneys and therefore the skin, as well as giving you healthy hair and nails. Watermelon is high in potassium and zinc and the seeds rich in vitamin E. If you are juicing for fun rather than for health, experiment with other varieties as their tastes all differ.

As most of the nutrients are to be found in the rind of the melon, it just requires chopping before juicing. To select a ripe watermelon, tap it with your knuckles and it should sound hollow. Ripe cantaloupes should yield to the pressure from your thumb at the stem end.

nectarines

Related to the peach, nectarines have a more colourful flesh and a smoother skin but are equally rich in folic acid, vitamin C, the B vitamins and have a smattering of assorted minerals. Nectarine juice can be very thick so is best mixed with other fruits – remove the stone before juicing.

QUICK TIP

*Always remove the stones from cherries, peaches,
nectarines, plums and apricots before adding the chopped
flesh to the juicer.*

oranges

Not only do oranges contain vitamin C, but also B vitamins, calcium,
potassium and magnesium. As with other citrus fruits, the nutrient-
dense part of the fruit is the pith, so peeling carefully before juicing to
retain the pith helps to ensure all the nutrients you can.

Choose large oranges that are firm and heavy for their size and have
a fine-textured skin. Five to six oranges will give about 600ml (1 pint)
of juice.

papaya

Nutritionally the papaya is rich in vitamin C and beta-carotene, which
the body converts to vitamin A – great for boosting the immunity. It
also contains an enzyme called papain, which helps to improve
digestion, especially with complex proteins such as meat.

The juice from these fruits is very thick so needs to be mixed with
other fruits. Remove the seeds before juicing.

basic ingredients

39

peaches

Peaches are part of the Prunus family, as are nectarines, prunes, plums and apricots. Their nutritional qualities are virtually the same as nectarines and are an ideal food for anybody with raised cholesterol or high blood pressure.

Peach juice can be very thick so is best mixed with other juices, poured over ice or blended into a smoothie. Remove the stone before juicing.

pears

Pears contain the soluble fibre pectin. They also provide a reasonable amount of vitamins A, C and E, as well as the mineral potassium.

There are a number of varieties of pears, so experiment to find your favourite taste and sweetness. Pear juice oxidises very quickly so should be drunk immediately. It is also very thick so is best mixed with other juices, but you will get lots of juice from a perfectly ripe pear.

pineapple

Pineapple contains the enzyme bromelain which has anti-inflammatory properties and has been found to be beneficial against conditions such as arthritis, urinary infections and sinus problems. Bromelain is found in the highest concentrations in the rind of the pineapple, so buy an organic fruit that will not need peeling to get the most nutrients from your juice.

Pineapples stop ripening the minute they are harvested, so buy your pineapple ripe – the fruit should be very heavy, which means it's juicy, and should smell sweet.

plums

A substance in the skin of plums stimulates movement of the bowels, hence prunes are normally eaten to help constipation. Plums contain a good level of vitamin C. Different varieties of plum will give differing flavours and sweetness, so experiment until you find the ones you prefer. Always remove the stone before juicing.

✔ **QUICK TIP**
Buy fruits and vegetables when there is a glut of them, or maybe you have a wonderful fruit tree or vegetable garden that is bursting with produce – that is the time your juicer will come into its own.

basic ingredients

pomegranate

The pomegranate has become very popular, with lots of studies confirming its beneficial qualities in health. It has high levels of cancer-fighting antioxidants as well as phytochemicals (plant chemicals) and minerals that help the fight against heart disease and circulation problems.

The name pomegranate comes from the French for 'seeded apple' and this is obvious when you cut into one. The seeds and flesh can be scooped out with a spoon and can be used for juicing or smoothies. When buying pomegranates, the heavier the fruit the better as this indicates more seeds.

raspberries

One of the great antioxidants needed to fight all the free radicals in our bodies, the raspberry is packed with vitamin C, beta-carotene and calcium, magnesium, phosphorus and sodium. It also tastes amazing and can transform any drink into a burst of summer.

Although great for smoothies, rasberries also make superb juice, which can be used for wonderful summer cocktails, either with or without alcohol! If you have a glut of them in the summer months they freeze very well.

redcurrants

Full of vitamin C, redcurrants are actually part of the gooseberry family. They also contain a little iron and are thought to be good for the immune system. Redcurrants have a short season and are best bought fresh. They can sometimes be rather tart so are best blended with sweeter fruit or vegetables. They give juices a great colour.

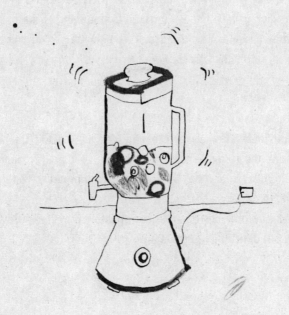

strawberries

A great source of vitamin C (more than citrus fruits), the strawberry is also a source of ellagic acids. The soluble fibre pectin, can also be found in these wonderful fruits, along with great antioxidants for cell protection. Their iron content is easily absorbed due to the high level of vitamin C.

Strawberries are now available all year round, but for a small, tender, great-tasting fruit be patient and wait for the summer season. The juice from strawberries will be quite thick, so either serve with mineral water or mixed with other juices. Remove the stalk and any leaves before juicing.

tomatoes

Tomatoes are extremely rich in antioxidants, making them good at protecting the cardiovascular system. The carotenoid lycopene, found in ripe tomatoes, also has anti-carcinogenic properties, with particular benefits for prostate cancer.

Try to buy organic tomatoes, or at least spray-free. Growing your own is not difficult in a grow bag.

vegetables

Most pure vegetable juices will need a little help on the sweetness front, so adding apples, oranges, or pineapple juice is normally a good basis for making a green juice palatable.

As with all produce, it is best to buy organic if you possibly can, as this cuts down on the amount of toxins you will take into your body. It also means you really do not have to peel anything but always wash produce well before preparation.

You will yield a higher quantity of juice if you roll green leaves into a ball before feeding into the juicer.

green juice
All dark green vegetables, like broccoli, cabbage, spinach, etc., contain something called chlorophyll, which absorbs light from the sun and turns it into energy. They are therefore a great source of energy, but unfortunately don't taste that great on their own! Try mixing a little green juice with some tasty fruits – you will still get the benefits but probably enjoy the juice more.

Always mix green juices, and beet juice, with others as they are very potent on their own and very strong in flavour. Mix with sweeter ingredients such as carrot or apple.

asparagus

A natural chemical called asparagines, found in asparagus, has a powerful diuretic effect – you will recognise this by the smell and the frequency of urinating within 30 minutes of eating it! It is also rumoured to be good for rheumatism as it breaks up oxalic acid crystals.

The flavour of asparagus is far superior when eaten in season. To prepare, don't worry about breaking off the woody stem – put it all in.

avocados

Avocados have had bad press for years, with many people believing that they are fattening. In fact, the fat they contain is the healthy monounsaturated, heart-protecting kind. They also contain starch, vitamins A, B, C and E and potassium, with a little protein thrown in, too.

basic ingredients

Avocados do not juice well, but are great for blending with other juices to make delicious and nutritious smoothies. Remove the stone and spoon out the flesh. Adding lemon or lime juice will prevent oxidation happening too quickly.

 TIP

To ripen avocados, place them in a brown paper bag at room temperature and they should ripen within a few days.

beetroot

An excellent source of iron, beetroot also contains the carotenoid betaine, which has numerous benefits including antioxidant properties. It is a powerful blood cleanser and tonic.

If you buy organic or grow your own, just scrub the skins, but if not then they are best peeled. Do not drink beetroot juice by itself as it is very potent, and don't drink too much if you have sugar problems. Don't panic if your urine is pink after drinking beet juice – this is perfectly normal!

basic ingredients

broccoli

Broccoli has been called one of the 'superfoods' as it has so much going for it – lots of fibre, is rich in vitamins A and C, and it has been shown to have protective properties against cancer. By cooking broccoli, even lightly steaming, you start to lose some of these great nutrients, and eating it raw is quite hard for the body to digest, so juicing is perfect.

Always look for broccoli that is dark green in colour and not limp. As this is a green juice, it is best mixed with other juices. Don't throw away the stalk – use every little bit!

brussels sprouts

Yes, believe it or not they can be juiced! And if that is the only way to get one past your lips then do give it a go as they are packed with nutrients including anti-cancer compounds and folate. No need to even chop these, just feed them in!

cabbage

A highly nutritious vegetable as well as inexpensive, cabbage offers great healing nutrients – vitamins C and B6, iron, folic acid, potassium, sulphur (great for chest infections or acne) and is widely known to be good for treating stomach ulcers.

Any variety of cabbage is great blended with carrot juice (think coleslaw in a glass!) As always with green juices, never drink too much as you may experience a feeling of gas or slight cramps in the intestine – just as if you had eaten too much cabbage – this is the sulphur resting in your stomach. Always blend with other juices.

To prepare, peel off the outer leaves and chop.

carrots

Carrots contain so much beta-carotene that one large carrot will provide enough vitamin A for the whole day. A powerful antioxidant, the carrot helps in the prevention of cancer, is anti-ageing, improves blood flow, and even helps in fighting diarrhoea. And of course, they help improve night vision (that's not an old wives' tale!)

Carrots are great for juicing as they blend well with lots of other fruit and vegetables and have a natural sweetness. Most of the nutrients in a carrot are found just under the skin, so wash instead of peeling. It helps if you cut off the tough tops, as they will gradually wear out your machine, and top and tail non-organic carrots. Look for hard carrots and store in the fridge to retain their moisture.

cauliflower

Full of potassium and phosphorus, it also supplies vitamins A and C, folic acid and iron, calcium and sulphur. Cauliflower is good when blended with other, sweeter juices. Cut off the outer leaves and some of the stalk as this part has a very strong taste, then just chop.

celery

Natural, organic sodium in celery is entirely soluble in water so less harmful to our bodies and in fact is needed for the health of the digestive system. Celery is over 95 per cent water, but it does contain some potassium which is good for the skin and helps to regulate blood pressure.

Always wash any soil from the ridges of the stalks before juicing. Celery juice is another staple ingredient that is great for livening up other juices. You can also use the leaves for juicing, or save them for decoration, especially if you are serving Bloody Marys or other cocktails.

cucumber

Another vegetable that is high in water content, the cucumber contains mineral salt that maintains healthy nails, skin and hair. It is also a natural diuretic and famously good for 'cooling'. Always buy firm, dark-skinned cucumbers and peel if they are waxed.

QUICK TIP

If you have a few pieces of fruit or vegetables in your kitchen that are not enough for a meal, they will more often than not make a great juice, cutting down on waste and boosting your health at the same time.

fennel

Both a vegetable and herb (the top fronds can be used separately) fennel is known for its properties as a detoxifier and an aid to digestion. It is sometimes used as a diuretic and is great for relieving trapped wind. If you love the flavour of aniseed you will love this vegetable. Always mix with other juices.

garlic

The list of therapeutic effects of garlic would take up half this book – it has been used medicinally for years. Probably its best-known use is as a blood thinner and is used to treat cardiovascular and heart problems.

Never drink garlic juice by itself and only juice one clove at a time as it is very potent. Always put the garlic in the juicer before the other ingredients to prevent your juicer from smelling forever – hopefully the ingredients following it will cleanse the juicer a little.

Buy garlic that is quite firm and store at room temperature. Remove the papery skin before juicing.

horseradish

Until recently it was impossible to get fresh horseradish unless you lived in the country and knew where to dig it up! More recently it has been stocked by some of the major supermarkets. Be warned, it is much stronger than the creamed horseradish you may have been adding to your Sunday roast beef, so add it in small amounts initially!

kale

Kale is part of the brassica family, along with cabbage and broccoli. It is great for providing energy and is very cleansing. Combine it with other ingredients.

lettuce

Rich in chlorophyll, lettuce helps to purify the blood and improve the appearance of your skin. Different varieties will give differing amounts of juice and even different flavours, so experiment with them all.

As with all leafy green vegetables, it is best to roll a few leaves together into a tight ball to ensure maximum juice.

parsnips

The great winter parsnip provides fibre, folic acid, potassium, vitamin E, B vitamins and traces of other minerals, which makes them great for helping to achieve healthy skin. They may also be of benefit for asthma sufferers.

This is one vegetable that should only be eaten in season. Look for organic, creamy-coloured, firm parsnips that are quite heavy. Top and tail before juicing and blend with other juices.

 QUICK TIP

Always remove tough stalks or ends from vegetables such as parsnips or carrots, and discard the stalks of peppers. This will prevent your juicer blade from wearing down quickly.

peppers

Another vegetable that is rich in vitamin C, with more than twice the amount contained in an orange. The vitamin C content changes as the pepper changes colour, starting at green with the lowest amount and ending at red, with three times the amount of vitamin C. Red and yellow varieties also provide beta-carotene and other antioxidants which makes them good for boosting the immune system.

Green peppers are rather bitter, even when cooked, so it's best to use red, orange or yellow ones. Always look for firm, heavy peppers and keep them in the fridge. Cut off the stalk, but leave the seeds.

radishes

Known to be good for gall bladder and liver problems, radishes contain calcium, potassium, sulphur, folic acid, vitamin C and selenium. However, they should be treated with caution as their hot, peppery flavour can be a problem to people suffering with ulcers or any type of gastric inflammatory disorder and they should not be eaten by anybody with thyroid problems.

Buy radishes that feel heavy – this will ensure they are at their freshest – and juice them as soon as possible, before they become 'woody' and their flavour intensifies. All types of radish can be juiced and their tops are nutritious too, so don't chop them off.

spinach

Spinach is actually very high in folic acid rather than iron and contains lots of protective carotenoids, some of which may help against failing eyesight. Wash well before juicing to remove any dirt or grit from the leaves. Spinach is a green juice and would not be very tasty drunk on its own – apart from anything else you would need a huge amount of it to make one glass!

sweet potatoes

Sweet potatoes are great for slow-release energy. They are full of phytochemicals including beta-carotene (hence their colour). It is surprising to think that a potato can be juiced, but they work surprisingly well. Just peel, chop and feed into the juicer.

watercress

Great for fighting off chest and urinary infections, as it acts as a natural antibiotic, watercress is very rich in vitamin C and B vitamins, and provides lots of energy.

Watercress has a great peppery taste but as with other green juices, make sure you mix it or dilute it with water. To get the most out of the leaves, roll them into a tight ball and feed into the machine whilst it is switched off.

herbs

If you only have what you think are a few unadventurous ingredients, adding herbs and spices is the easiest way to liven them up. And on top of that they will add yet more nutrients, giving you even more goodness.

There are lots of fresh herbs available in supermarkets or farmers' markets and it is very easy to grow your own. Herbs are ideally suited to pots and containers, so even if all you have is a window box then it's time to get your green fingers to work! It is far more satisfying, and healthy, to pick your herbs off the bush rather than the supermarket shelf.

basil

This is the main ingredient of that wonderful Italian sauce, pesto. Basil is not only a great flavour to add to any tomato-based food or drink: it is also full of medicinal properties that aid digestion and is said to be antiseptic. There are lots of varieties too – purple, Thai, lemon, and peppermint, among many others.

Roll the leaves into a tight ball before putting into the feeder, to gain more juice.

coriander

This strong aromatic herb is widely used in Indian and Thai cooking and has been used in Asian folk medicine to treat stomach problems, fevers, colds and even hernias. It is rich in vitamins A, B and C as well as a few minerals. The leaves, stalks and roots can be used in cooking. For juicing just use the leaves and stalks.

Roll into a tight ball before putting into the juicer to ensure maximum juice yield.

mint

The smell of freshly picked mint is the quintessential scent of summer. Its soothing properties that aid digestion make it a herb worth having in the kitchen. It is probably the easiest herb to grow, although it will take over your garden if you don't keep it contained. There are many different mints, including peppermint, spearmint, Pennyroyal and basil mint.

For juicing, both the leaves and stalk can be used.

parsley

As with all green juices, this one definitely needs diluting with other juices or with water – it is very strong, but certainly very healthy. Full of chlorophyll, the green pigment in plants that traps the energy of

basic ingredients

sunlight, parsley is also rich in iron. Flat-leaf parsley makes a more potent juice than curly, so experiment with both.

Unless you have a masticating machine, you need to pack the leaves very tightly into the feeder, or in between another fruit like apples, to get the maximum yield.

rosemary

Both a tonic and a stimulant, rosemary is said to improve memory loss and reduce nervous tension. It also acts as a good insect repellant. It does have quite a strong flavour so experiment with quantities.

spices

Spices are aromatic seasonings generally characterised by strong, pungent flavours. They are derived from:

• Fruits (chilli, pepper, allspice)

• Seeds (cardamom, cumin, nutmeg)

• Roots (ginger, turmeric, horseradish)

- Flower buds (capers, cloves)

- Bark of tropical plants (cinnamon)

Spices also help to give a kick to some drinks – a little cinnamon or nutmeg sprinkled over apple juice can change the flavour completely. Use your spices regularly and always make sure they are within their use-by date to ensure a strong flavour.

Most spices are dried and are best sprinkled on your finished juice rather than in the juicer, with the exception of fresh ginger.

chilli

Depending on how hot you like your food, or in this case, juices, adding chillies is all down to personal taste. Just be wary of which chillies you choose as some are much hotter than others. As a general rule, the smaller they are the more potent they will be! Red chillies are also normally hotter as they have had longer to ripen.

cinnamon

Cinnamon is obtained from the inner bark of a tropical Asian tree and has been used in Chinese medicine for hundreds of years. It contains, iron, calcium, manganese and vitamin C. It is used mainly for the digestion and has a mild anti-inflammatory effect. Sprinkled over juices, it can change the flavour enormously.

cloves

A clove is actually an unopened aromatic flower bud of a tree of the eucalyptus family. Their English name actually derived from the Latin word clavus, which means nail, due to their shape. In recent studies extracts of cloves were found to help with the effects of balancing blood sugar in people suffering with diabetes.

Cloves have a very warm, aromatic taste and make a wonderful addition to both sweet and savoury dishes or juices.

ginger

Ginger has been used medicinally for hundreds of years. It benefits arthritis, rheumatism and other inflammatory conditions, travel sickness and morning sickness, along with coughs, colds and bronchitis.

You cannot beat the flavour of fresh ginger root for spicing up juices – it will turn a boring apple and carrot juice into a cocktail! You do not need to peel ginger root. Preserved stem ginger can also be used.

lemon grass

Another more recent addition to our supermarket shelves, lemon grass is a wonderful herb to use in juices as it adds a great lemon flavour but is much sweeter than the citrus flavour gained from lemons. Oils and teas made from lemon grass have been used medicinally for a number of ailments.

nutmeg

In Indian Ayurvedic medicine, nutmeg is believed to promote healthy skin and can help coughs and nausea. Freshly grated nutmeg is preferable to ground as it will hold its flavour for longer.

unusual ingredients

There are a few ingredients that have become well known purely because of juicing – you may have heard of wheatgrass even if you haven't tried it. Most of these ingredients are put in juices purely for health reasons, hardly ever for their taste!

alfalfa sprouts

Sprouts are a great way of getting your daily nutrients in a small package! They contain concentrated amounts of phytochemicals that protect us against disease, as well as plant oestrogens that are helpful in controlling the symptoms of PMS or the menopause. They are also full of antioxidants that protect us against the onset of ageing, amongst other things. See page 23 for information on sprouting your own alfalfa and other beans and seeds – a great way of ensuring a ready supply.

aloe vera

Aloe vera is well known for its skin-healing properties but the juice also has health benefits for improvement in skin condition, digestion, the immune system and inflammatory disorders. The inner gel of the leaves contains antioxidants, minerals, amino acids, anti-inflammatory enzymes, plus other nutrients that have a healthy impact on the body. It is possible to grow your own plant but organic aloe vera juice is available from most health-food stores and on the internet. This can then be added to your own freshly made juices.

honey

A great way to sweeten juices is to add a tiny amount of honey, but don't kid yourself that this is healthier than adding sugar as it's not – honey has just the same effect on the body as sugar does but it is more natural. Always buy organic and unblended honey for the best flavour and to ensure it has not been treated in any way.

omega oils

Omega oils are essential fatty acids that maintain healthy skin, heart and brains. They are also vital for hormone balance, nerves, sleep and can help to combat depression. Adding oils to your juices may not be the tastiest way but it certainly is better than not getting them at all. There is a huge variety of oils available now, with differing quantities of omega 3, 6 and 9, and despite the memories you may have of being forced to swallow fishy cod liver oil, the latest oils are tasteless and odourless. Shop around to find the best-quality oil for the amount you can afford.

basic ingredients

spirulina

Spirulina is a blue-green alga that is said to contain the most remarkable concentration of nutrients ever known to be grown in any plant, grain or herb. It is cultivated around the world and is now used as a dietary supplement, either as a tablet or powder.

Spirulina is a complete protein, containing all the essential amino acids our body needs as well as essential fatty acids (omega 3 and omega 6), B vitamins, vitamins C and E, and an even longer long list of minerals including calcium, magnesium, selenium, zinc and manganese. The health benefits include increased energy, help in detoxification and a boost to the immune system.

Sprinkle the powder into juices or smoothies, following the recommended dosage on the packet.

wheatgrass

Wheatgrass has been called a superfood and may help by fortifying the blood, removing toxins, nourishing the liver and kidneys, cleansing the lymph system and basically restoring vitality. A 25g (1oz) dose of wheatgrass is said to have the equivalent vitamin and mineral content of over 1kg (2lb) of vegetables. It is full of phytonutrients, antioxidants, amino acids (for building protein), vitamins B, C, E and K, folic acid, beta-carotene, calcium, zinc, selenium, magnesium… and the list goes on.

Wheatgrass is an acquired taste and does have the side effect of 'repeating' slightly throughout the day. It is not easy to grow in large quantities at home but can be bought from the internet, either pre-cut in bags or still growing, in trays, ready to harvest.

Note Before buying wheatgrass make sure your juicer is capable of juicing wheatgrass – see 'Finding the machine for you', page 15.

recipes for health

- Start Juicing

- Fresh is Best

- Energy and Power Juices

- Vitamin Boosters

- Ailment Helpers

start juicing

If you fancy a drink, simply open your fridge, choose a selection of tasty fruits and vegetables, and blitz them into a refreshing, nutrient-packed beverage. You will be amazed at the wonderful cocktails you will come up with and you'll rarely repeat the same one twice!

One of the great things about juice recipes is that you don't really need them! You can juice pretty much anything, and mixing and experimenting is all part of the fun. However, if you're new to juicing then a recipe is the best place to start – after that just try different combinations and you will soon find some of your own favourites.

The other exciting part of the juicing experience is that you don't have to weigh anything – recipes can't go wrong: they may just taste sweeter or sharper depending on what you mix together.

The following recipes provide juice for one serving, unless otherwise stated, so to increase quantities simply increase your ingredients in proportion, not exceeding the capacity of your juicer.

hints for taste perfection

If something you have made is not sweet enough, just add an apple or two, carrots or a handful of grapes – they are sweet, nutritious and seem to mix well with lots of other fruit and vegetables.

If a vegetable juice is too green (and they can sometimes seem a little like drinking cold cabbage soup!), just add a fruit of your choice to bring in the sweetness and flavour again, or a piece of ginger to spice it up.

Always stir your juice before drinking, as the flavours of the ingredients will be in the layers you fed them into the machine. If you leave the juice for only a few minutes it will start to separate so give it another stir to bring it back together again.

✔ QUICK TIP

When you find a combination of ingredients that you really love, write it down so you will know how to do it again – after making a few of these you will find it hard to remember what you put in each one!

fresh is best

It is really important to drink your juice while it is fresh. The longer you leave it the less nutrients there will be – the juicing process starts to break everything down and then the enzymes continue the job. Nutrients are sensitive to air, heat and light and these will all cause the juice to start breaking down. When a juice starts to change colour that is a sign of oxidation or the juice going bad – time to pour it away. Some juices oxidise more quickly than others – apple will always oxidise faster than citrus fruits.

It's hard to put a time on when or how quickly you should drink your juice, but try to imagine how soon an apple turns brown when you slice into it – oxidation starts immediately and gradually the nutrients are deteriorating. So in essence I would suggest you drink your juice as soon as you have made it. If you have to leave it for 30 minutes then give it a stir and enjoy it anyway – it will still be more beneficial than a glass of fizzy pop!

storing and transporting

If you can't drink your juice instantly or you would like to be able to take it to work or school, you can minimise the loss of nutrients.

Invest in a small bullet flask that will fit into your freezer. Place the flask in the freezer at least an hour before making your juice (or overnight if you want to make it at breakfast). As soon as you have made your juice pour it into the flask and put the lid on. The cold and lack of air should help to slow down the rate of oxidation and keep your juice fresher for longer. Adding a little lemon juice will slow down the rate of oxidation.

> ✔ **QUICK TIP**
> *If you have an excess of one fruit or vegetable and you don't want to waste it, try juicing it and pouring into an ice cube tray. Every time you make a smoothie just pop a couple of ice cubes into the blender and you have another flavour and more nutrients added to your drink.*

I would never suggest keeping anything in the freezer for longer than one month. Only freeze juices that you may use in cooking or in smoothies, not just to be drunk on their own. Freeze in ice blocks so you can pop them into your recipes when required (see page 103 or page 107 for recipes using ginger or garlic juice).

energy and power juices

All recipes serve one unless otherwise stated.

Choosing ingredients that are good for energy is easy when using fresh fruit and vegetables as most are nutrient-packed to start with. The following recipes combine ingredients that contain vitamins which give a real boost to energy, and these include watercress, courgettes, asparagus, lettuce, peppers, cauliflower, cabbage, strawberries and tomatoes – and that's just for starters! Mixed with other great fruits and vegetables that give delicious flavour and even more nutrients to increase iron levels or boost your metabolism, you'll be buzzing around all day.

super seven

This juice has seven great energy-building vegetables, along with lots of antioxidants to fight off infections. By combining beetroot with other vegetables you get all of its benefits without the potency of pure juice.

> **2 carrots**
> **1 sweet potato**
> **1 handful of broccoli, florets and stalks**
> **1/2 small beetroot**
> **1/4 red pepper**
> **1 tomato**
> **1/4 cucumber**

- *Chop all the ingredients.*
- *Juice all the ingredients and mix well before drinking.*

muscle builder

To build muscle your body needs protein, which you would normally get from things like chicken, fish and nuts. We can also get protein from vegetables, and broccoli is good for almost everything – it is a true 'superfood'. Like all green juices, mix it with other things and don't have too much in one day.

> **2 carrots**
> **2 handfuls of spinach**
> **1 handful of broccoli, florets and stalks**
> **1 handful of grapes**

- *Chop the carrots.*
- *Squeeze the spinach leaves into a tight ball and pack between the carrots, broccoli and grapes.*
- *Juice the ingredients and mix well before drinking.*

spiral wonder

Adding spirulina to any juice will beef up your nutrients as it's considered to be one of the most concentrated plant foods in existence.

> **1 apple**
> **2 carrots**
> **2 kiwi fruit**
> **1 mango**
> **1 handful of broccoli, florets and stalks**
> **1/2 tsp spirulina powder**

- *Chop the apple, carrots and kiwi fruit.*
- *Peel, stone and chop the mango.*
- *Juice the apple, carrots, kiwi fruit, mango and broccoli.*
- *Sprinkle in the spirulina powder and mix well before drinking.*

water express

Watercress is full of B vitamins as well as vitamin C, and can even work as a natural antibiotic, helping to keep your gut flora healthy.

1 apple
2 celery stalks
2 handfuls of baby spinach leaves
1 handful of watercress

- *Chop the apple and celery.*
- *Roll the spinach and watercress leaves into tight ball.*
- *Juice all the ingredients and mix well before drinking.*

cauli wobbles

Cauliflower has an unusual but distinctive flavour and should always be mixed with other ingredients.

> $1/3$ small cauliflower, florets and stalk
> 1 apple
> 1 orange
> 1 kiwi fruit
> 1 handful of baby spinach leaves
> 1 stick of lemon grass

- *Chop the cauliflower and apple.*
- *Peel the orange, leaving on as much white pith as possible, then chop.*
- *Chop the kiwi fruit, peeled if preferred.*
- *Juice all the ingredients and mix well before drinking.*

recipes for health

kale and hearty

Kale is quite a strong flavour so requires some apples to sweeten it up. It can be substituted with spring greens, Savoy cabbage or even Chinese cabbage.

2 handfuls of kale leaves
$1/2$ cucumber
2 celery stalks
3 apples
2cm (1in) piece of fresh root ginger

- *Roll the kale leaves into a tight ball before juicing to ensure maximum juice yield.*
- *Peel and chop the cucumber.*
- *Juice all the ingredients and mix well before drinking.*

vitamin boosters

All recipes serve one unless otherwise stated.

Pretty much all juices boost your vitamin intake and any that have vitamins A, C and E could also be classed as antioxidants (along with the minerals zinc and selenium). These are well known for their healing properties, helping the immune system to fight off infections and fighting the free radicals that age us – all of that just in one juice!

breakfast zing

Starting the day with a citrus-based juice is always a great way to wake up your taste buds and your body. Blueberries are one of best fruits for antioxidants to help with anti-ageing and keeping your skin looking healthy. The sweet aniseed flavour of fennel is subtle in this juice – add more if you are a real aniseed fan.

> **1 pink or white grapefruit**
> **1/2 medium fennel bulb**
> **1 small handful of blueberries**
> **8 grapes**

- *Peel the grapefruit leaving on as much white pith as possible.*
- *Chop the grapefruit and fennel.*
- *Juice all the ingredients and mix well before drinking.*

berry treat

A real summer favourite, when all the berries are at their best and full of flavour (and antioxidants). For a longer summer drink, mix the juice with sparkling water and pour over ice.

1 handful of cherries
1 handful of strawberries, tops removed
1 handful of raspberries
1 handful of blueberries

- *Stone the cherries.*
- *Juice all the ingredients and mix well before drinking.*

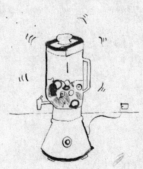

crabbage

Cranberries are known for their therapeutic qualities for helping with the symptoms of cystitis. This pure juice may seem a little sharp – experiment with the number of apples and apricots, depending on how sweet you like your drinks. If you need an extra sweetener, stir in a teaspoon of honey.

> 2 apricots
> 2 apples
> 1/8 Savoy cabbage
> 2cm (1in) piece of fresh root ginger
> 1 small handful of cranberries (defrosted if frozen)

- *Stone and chop the apricots.*
- *Chop the apple and cabbage.*
- *Juice all the ingredients and mix well before drinking.*

green dream

This juice contains lots of greens to help the liver detoxify as well as giving antioxidants and iron. It is very strong and not to everybody's taste – if you prefer your juices a little sweeter, just add an apple or two.

3 carrots
1 celery stalk
2 big handfuls of spinach
1 big handful of lettuce (Romaine is good)
1 small handful of flat-leaf parsley

- *Chop the carrots and celery.*
- *Roll the spinach leaves into a tight ball.*
- *Juice all the ingredients and mix well before drinking.*

mid-morning pick-me-up

Parsley gives very strong juice so use in moderation and experiment with the amount – flat-leaf is also stronger than the curly variety. It is rich in iron so your blood will appreciate the boost.

> **4 carrots**
> **1 small handful of flat-leaf parsley**
> **2 handfuls of spinach**
> **2 celery stalks**
> **1 apple**

- *Chop the carrots.*
- *Wrap the parsley and spinach leaves into a tight ball and feed between the carrot and celery. Juice together.*
- *Add the apple and juice the ingredients together. Mix well before drinking.*

recipes for health

pepper rainbow

Peppers are one of the greatest vegetables for getting your fill of antioxidants. This juice has every colour going! There is no need to remove the seeds from the pepper but always remove the stalk, to save the wear and tear on your machine.

1 red pepper
1 yellow pepper
1 orange pepper
1 orange
1 small handful of fresh mint leaves
a few leaves of flat-leaf parsley

- *Chop all the peppers, removing the stalks.*
- *Peel the orange, leaving as much white pith as possible.*
- *Juice everything together and mix well before drinking.*

bone shaker

Healthy bones and cartilage need vitamin C, calcium and other minerals, which are found in root vegetables. They also need vitamin D, which is found in oysters, so if you dare, pop a raw oyster in your juice for a great start to the day – it will also provide you with lots of zinc to boost your sex life!

> **1/2 small turnip**
> **3 carrots**
> **3 broccoli florets**
> **2 apples**
> **2cm (1in) piece of fresh root ginger**
> **fresh oyster (optional)**

- *Chop the turnip, carrots, broccoli and apple.*
- *Juice all the fruit and vegetables, mix well and add the oyster, if using, before drinking.*

ruby anyday

Redcurrants can sometimes be a little sharp, but blended here with sweet carrot juice and the spiciness of ginger, they add great flavour, as well as a gorgeous colour.

 QUICK TIP

Eat a redcurrant or two before you juice them to get an idea of their sweetness – this should help you decide how many to add for the sweetness of your juice.

2 medium carrots
1 handful of blueberries
1 handful of grapes
1 small handful of redcurrants
1 small knob of fresh ginger

- *Chop the carrots.*
- *Juice all the ingredients and mix well before drinking.*

veggie boost

Carrots, beetroot and celery don't really need any sweetening, but adding apple and pear to the mix really gives a great sweet flavour, with lots of healthy vitamins, too. This juice is a perfect way of getting those vital vitamins in and helping towards your five-a-day quota.

1/2 **fresh beetroot**
1 **apple**
1 **pear**
2 **carrots**
2 **celery stalks**

- *Chop all the fruit and vegetables and juice together.*
- *Mix well before drinking.*

skin refresher

Cantaloupe melon is great for your skin and in Asia figs are revered as one of the most aphrodisiac of foods, so after this juice it may be more than your skin that is refreshed! The kumquats give an intense orange flavour even though they don't produce much juice.

1/2 small cantaloupe melon
8 kumquats
2 figs

- *Chop the melon, including the skin and seeds.*
- *Juice all the ingredients and mix well before drinking.*

vit c dream

When everybody around you has a cold you need to boost your vitamin C levels to help your immune system fight off any infections.

12 cherries
1 orange
1 apple
12 strawberries, tops removed

- *Remove the stones from the cherries.*
- *Peel the orange, leaving as much of the white pith as possible.*
- *Juice all the ingredients together and mix well before drinking.*

minty sunrise

Full of vitamin C and beta-carotene, this drink has the added flavour of summer with the zing of fresh mint – use as little or as much as you like for added mintiness.

2 carrots
1 orange
6 grapes
1 small handful of fresh mint, leaves and stalk

- *Chop the carrots.*
- *Peel the orange, leaving as much white pith as possible, then chop.*
- *Juice all the ingredients together and mix well before drinking.*

pepper delight

If you expect red peppers to be bitter or sharp then this juice will change your mind – mixed with apple and orange juice they are so sweet and the juice is the most fantastic colour. This is a great juice to boost your immune system.

1 orange
1 red pepper
1 apple

- *Peel the orange, leaving on as much white pith as possible, and then chop.*
- *Remove the stalk of the red pepper and then chop – don't worry about taking the seeds out.*
- *Chop the apple.*
- *Juice all the ingredients together and mix well before drinking.*

lemony melody

Lemon grass is a great addition to most juices – it adds the lemon flavour without adding any sharpness. However, it is quite tough and may get caught in the machine so watch closely.

> **3 apricots**
> **1 kiwi fruit**
> **2 carrots**
> **1 apple**
> **1 handful of blueberries**
> **1 stick of lemon grass**

- *Stone and chop the apricots.*
- *Chop the kiwi fruit and remove the peel if preferred.*
- *Chop the carrots and apple.*
- *Juice all the ingredients and mix well before drinking.*

ailment helpers

All recipes serve one unless otherwise stated.

Juices are not just for health, but they can certainly help when you need a boost of a certain vitamin, mineral, antioxidant or cocktail of all of them. The fact that your body does not have to fight through all the fibre of the fruit or vegetable means that the nutrients will be absorbed into your bloodstream that much faster – getting to work on your symptoms as soon as possible.

toxic overload

Help your body to detox once in a while by drinking fresh juices and cutting out stimulants (tea, coffee, alcohol) and unhealthy foods (chips, takeaways). If your body is really overloaded with toxins you can normally tell by the condition of your skin. The best time to start is when the new season fruit and vegetables hit the shelves in the spring, and combine fruit and vegetables with those that have specific detox properties, such as the brassica family (cabbage, broccoli, Brussels sprouts) plus nuts, seeds, peppers and citrus fruits (not grapefruit). Here are a couple of recipes to get you started.

DETOX 1

1/4 Savoy cabbage
2 oranges
2 apricots
2 kiwi fruits

- Chop the cabbage.
- Peel and chop the orange, leaving as much white pith as possible.
- Stone and chop the apricots.
- Chop the kiwi fruits, peeling them if preferred.
- Juice all the ingredients and mix well before drinking.

DETOX 2

1 orange
1/4 small cabbage
1 handful of broccoli, florets and stalks
1/3 small cantaloupe melon

- Peel the orange, leaving as much white pith as possible.
- Chop the remaining ingredients, and juice together.
- Mix well before drinking.

travel sickness

Ginger has always been known to be good for calming the stomach and helping with nausea. This may also be worth trying if you are pregnant and suffering with morning sickness – it is quite safe and there are no side-effects. This can also be served diluted with mineral water or poured over ice.

2 apples
1 kiwi fruit
3cm (1¹/2in) piece of fresh root ginger

- *Chop the apples.*
- *Peel and chop the kiwi fruit.*
- *Juice the ingredients and mix well before drinking.*

headaches and migraine

Getting nutrients into your system quickly when you have a headache or migraine is of vital importance and juices are perfect. Wheatgerm is rich in magnesium which is good for relaxing muscles and has been known to help in the treatment of migraines.

> **2 apples**
> **1/2 Romaine lettuce**
> **1/2 fennel bulb**
> **1/2 lemon**
> **1 tsp wheatgerm**

- *Chop the apples, lettuce and fennel.*
- *Roll the lettuce leaves into tight balls to ensure maximum juice yield.*
- *Peel the lemon, leaving as much white pith as possible.*
- *Juice the apples, lettuce, fennel and lemon.*
- *Stir in the wheatgerm and serve immediately.*

cystitis

Drinking lots of liquids can help relieve the symptoms of cystitis and cranberries are also known to help.

1 large wedge of watermelon, including pips
¹/₂ cucumber
1 small handful of cranberries
sprig or two of fresh mint

- *Chop the watermelon, including the skin.*
- *Peel the cucumber and chop.*
- *Juice the ingredients and mix well before drinking.*

anti-inflammatory

Arthritis is an inflammatory condition so it is important to avoid foods that may cause inflammation. Fruits and vegetables that are best avoided include: all citrus fruits, all nightshade family of vegetables (tomatoes, potatoes, aubergines, red, yellow and green peppers). Getting more essential fats into your diet will also help so, if you can bear it, a little fish oil in a juice may ease your aching joints.

> 1 handful of broccoli, florets and stalks
> 3 carrots
> 1/2 small beetroot
> 6 grapes
> 2cm (1in) piece of fresh root ginger
> 1 tsp fish oil (optional)

- *Chop the broccoli, carrots and beetroot.*
- *Juice the ingredients, stir in the fish oil if using and mix well before drinking.*

constipation

Long-term requirements are fibre, water and exercise – these will all help, but if you want to get things moving straight away try juices with prunes, dark leafy green vegetables and figs. Seek medical advice if the symptoms persist.

2 pears
2 handfuls of spinach
1 small handful of prunes
1 fig

- *Chop the pears.*
- *Roll the spinach leaves into a tight ball before juicing to ensure maximum yield of juice.*
- *Juice all the ingredients and mix well before drinking.*

acne

Bad digestion or a sluggish liver, too much sugar or not enough fibre and water, or smoking and pollution – these can all affect our skin.

Keep the liver healthy with cabbage and broccoli and kill off all the free radicals with antioxidants from fruits, especially berries.

3 carrots
1/2 Romaine lettuce
1 handful of spinach leaves
2 spears of asparagus
1 small handful of blueberries

- *Chop the carrots.*
- *Roll the lettuce and spinach leaves into a tight ball before juicing to ensure maximum yield of juice.*
- *Juice all the ingredients and mix well before drinking.*

VARIATION
1/2 cantaloupe melon
2 carrots
1 small handful of strawberries

- *Chop the cantaloupe and carrots.*
- *Juice all the ingredients and mix well before drinking.*

recipes with a twist

- Spice It Up!
- Hot Toddies
- Naughty But Nice

spice it up!

All recipes serve one unless otherwise stated.

Add some spice to any drink, be it juices, smoothies or cocktails, and it normally brings it to life. Fresh ginger is perfect for putting in the juicer but don't forget all the jars of dried spices you have in the cupboard too – sprinkle a few grains on the top of juices and experience the different flavours.

ginger whizz

Ginger is great for adding a real zing to any drink – it certainly adds some heat so be wary of adding too much. It's also good for arthritis sufferers or relieving symptoms of nausea.

> **1 lime**
> **3cm (1¹/₂in) piece of fresh root ginger**
> **2 carrots**
> **¹/₄ cantaloupe melon**

- *Peel the lime, leaving as much white pith as possible.*
- *Chop all the ingredients and juice together.*
- *Mix well before drinking.*

citrus morning

Citrus fruits are always good first thing in the morning – they have a real zing to them and with added fresh ginger they will definitely wake you up and get you starting the day with a skip in your step. Tangerines can be substituted with clementines or mandarins.

> 1 grapefruit
> 2 tangerines
> 2 oranges
> 2cm (1in) piece of fresh root ginger

- *Peel the grapefruit, tangerines and oranges, leaving on as much white pith as possible.*
- *Juice all the ingredients and mix well before drinking.*

spicy virgin mary

Fresh tomato juice is great with the kick of garlic and Tabasco – make this as strong as you like! Celery can be quite salty so check the taste before you season. Remember to juice the garlic first or push the cloves inside the tomatoes to prevent your machine from constantly smelling and tasting of garlic.

10 ripe tomatoes
3 celery stalks
1 small fennel bulb
2–3 cloves of garlic
1 shot of Tabasco
freshly milled black pepper

- Chop the tomatoes, celery and fennel. Peel the garlic.
- Juice the tomatoes, celery, fennel and cloves of garlic.
- Mix well and taste before adding Tabasco and freshly milled pepper.

recipes with a twist

ginger blender

This is not quite a smoothie but it is certainly a little more than a juice! If you like ginger you will love this sweet, spicy drink. Stem ginger is very strong and very sweet and adds a different flavour from fresh ginger.

3 apples
1 lemon
2 knobs of stem ginger with 1 tsp syrup from the jar

- *Chop the apples.*
- *Peel the lemon, leaving as much white pith on as possible.*
- *Juice two of the apples and the lemon.*
- *Pour the juice in a blender and add the remaining ingredients.*
- *Blend until smooth and serve.*

recipes with a twist

horsing around

Fresh horseradish can certainly give a punch – too much and it will also make your eyes water! Mixed with ginger and tomatoes in this non-alcoholic Bloody Mary, it will also provide lots of antioxidants to help fight off infections. If you want a little more excitement just add ice and vodka.

2 carrots
3 celery stalks
8 medium tomatoes
1 clove of garlic
2cm (1in) piece of fresh root ginger
2cm (1in) piece of fresh horseradish

- *Chop the carrots, celery and tomatoes. Peel the garlic.*
- *Juice all the ingredients together and mix well before drinking.*

clear head

You wouldn't think apples and carrots would be very exciting, but add a knob of ginger and the whole thing changes – add as little or as much as you like to vary the heat.

1 sharp eating apple
3 carrots
2cm (1in) piece of fresh root ginger

• *Chop the apple and carrots.*
• *Juice everything together and mix well before drinking.*

spiced water

This is a very simple juice but with lots of stimulation! Watermelon is very cooling and full of energy, and ginger is great for improving the digestion and circulation. Other varieties of melon could be used.

¹/₄ large watermelon
2cm (1in) piece of fresh root ginger

- *Chop the watermelon, including seeds and skin.*
- *Juice both ingredients and mix well before drinking.*

hot toddies

All recipes serve one unless otherwise stated.

Juices do not always have to be cold and refreshing – they can also be warm and comforting. Think of a soothing hot lemon and ginger tea, maybe with a drop of medicinal whisky.

✔ **QUICK TIP**
When warming, take care not to overheat the juice as this will start to destroy the nutrients. Bring the heat up gently and serve whilst warm.

ribina mania

Perfect for soothing a sore throat or just to comfort on a cold winter evening. You can use frozen fruits if making this out of season.

2 handfuls of blackcurrants (defrosted if frozen)
boiled hot water

- *Juice the blackcurrants into a mug.*
- *Pour over hot water that has boiled and been left to cool slightly.*
- *Stir well and drink whilst still warm.*

hot lemon and honey

This is perfect as the first line of defence against the onset of a cold, with vitamin C and soothing ginger, together with the antiseptic properties of honey. Omit the whisky if you prefer a non-alcoholic drink, or substitute it with your favourite tipple.

1 lemon
2cm (1in) piece of fresh root ginger
boiled hot water
$1/2$–1 tsp honey
a dash of whisky (optional)

- *Peel the lemon, leaving as much white pith as possible.*
- *Juice the lemon and ginger and pour into a mug.*
- *Top up with hot water and stir in the honey.*
- *Add a dash of whisky and drink while still warm.*

recipes with a twist

pear drops

Warm pear juice with a touch of spice from fresh ginger and cinnamon has a grown-up taste. Be sure to find ripe, soft pears to gain the most juice from them.

> **5 ripe pears, such as conference**
> **2cm (1in) piece of fresh root ginger**
> **a large pinch of ground cinnamon**

- *Chop the pears.*
- *Juice the pears and ginger.*
- *Pour the juice into a small pan and sprinkle in the ground cinnamon.*
- *Heat very gently and drink while still warm.*

recipes with a twist

brandied blackberry

A warming, soothing drink with lots of vitamin C and spices to pep you up! Perfect in autumn when there is an abundance of fresh blackberries growing in the hedgerows.

3 handfuls of blackberries
a pinch of ground nutmeg or cloves
a dash of brandy

- *Juice the blackberries and pour into a small saucepan.*
- *Heat very gently then pour into a glass or cup.*
- *Sprinkle over the spice and stir in the brandy.*
- *Drink while still warm.*

apple spice

Even freshly made apple juice can seem a little dull at times, but warming it up and sprinkling in a few spices will certainly change your view. Choose your favourite spice – cinnamon, nutmeg, cloves or even mixed spice – they all work very well.

5 apples
1/4 tsp ground cloves

- *Chop and juice the apples.*
- *Pour the juice into a small pan and sprinkle over the ground cloves.*
- *Warm gently, stirring occasionally.*
- *Drink while still warm.*

recipes with a twist

naughty but nice

All recipes serve one unless otherwise stated.

Juices are great for a healthy diet but they're also perfect for mixing with alcohol for making delicious cocktails. Think of all the cocktails you've ever had that had some kind of juice in them, then imagine how much nicer they would be made with fresh juice – now is your chance!

peach bellini
Serves 8

This is a great way to drink champagne and gives it a real summer twist for a special occasion. For extra punch you could add a little peach schnapps.

8 peaches
1 bottle of champagne

- *Stone the peaches before juicing.*
- *Divide the peach juice between 8 champagne glasses.*
- *Top up each glass with champagne and serve immediately.*

black cassis

Crème de cassis is lovely in a long drink with fresh blackcurrant juice and sparkling water (or lemonade it you want it sweeter). You could also use redcurrants but check the sweetness as they can be very sharp.

> **2 handfuls of blackcurrants**
> **a dash of crème de cassis**
> **ice**
> **sparkling water (or lemonade)**

- *Juice the blackcurrants.*
- *Add a dash of cassis and pour into a glass of ice.*
- *Top up with sparkling water or lemonade, stir and serve.*

 TIP
If you don't have enough juice to serve to unexpected guests, just top up with sparkling water and serve over ice for a great refreshing drink.

recipes with a twist

pina colada

This cocktail will have you dreaming of a tropical beach – fresh pineapple juice, fresh coconut milk and a splash of rum – pure heaven. It may seem like a lot of effort but if you have the ingredients to hand, it's worth it!

1 fresh coconut, or 400g (13oz) tin coconut milk
¹/₂ medium pineapple
a splash of light rum
ice

- *Make a hole in the two eyes of the coconut to enable you to drain out the water (a screwdriver and hammer are good for this). Put the coconut water to one side.*

- *Crack the coconut with the hammer – if you hit it along the seam it will break more easily.*

- *Break up the coconut flesh, don't worry about the rind, and feed into your juicer.*

- *When you have put through all the flesh pour in the water, which will rinse through the fibres that are left and give you coconut milk.*

- *Juice the pineapple and mix with the coconut milk.*

- *Add a splash of rum and serve poured over ice.*

recipes with a twist

blueberry martini

Another use for crème de cassis, this is one to impress your friends. It does require a cocktail shaker but failing that, mixing the drink in a jug with the ice and then straining it will work just as well.

> **1 handful of blueberries**
> **a shot of vodka**
> **a shot of crème de cassis**
> **ice**

- *Juice the blueberries.*
- *Pour the juice and the remaining ingredients into a cocktail shaker and shake well until blended and chilled.*
- *Strain into a Martini glass and serve.*

bloody mary

If you want a non-alcoholic version (a Virgin Mary), just leave out the vodka. As with all spicy drinks, taste it as you go rather than overdose on the heat.

> **3 tomatoes**
> **2 celery stalks**
> **1/4 small bulb of fennel**
> **a wedge of lemon**
> **a shot of vodka**
> **ice**
> **Tabasco, to taste**
> **Worcestershire sauce, to taste**

- *Chop the tomatoes, celery and fennel, and juice together with the lemon.*
- *Pour into an ice-filled glass.*
- *Add Tabasco and Worcestershire sauce to taste and stir well before drinking.*

recipes with a twist

darling clementine

This refreshing, fruity drink is just as tasty without the alcohol.

> **2 apples**
> **2 pears**
> **2 clementines (or satsumas)**
> **a dash of Cointreau**
> **ice**

- *Chop the apples and pears.*
- *Peel the clementines or satsumas, leaving as much white pith as possible.*
- *Juice the fruits together.*
- *Add a dash of Cointreau, pour over ice and serve.*

mango mojito

The mango gives this a twist on the normal Mojito to create a smooth, great-tasting drink.

> **2 mangoes**
> **1 lime**
> **1 small handful of mint leaves**
> **a dash of rum (white or dark)**
> **ice**

- *Peel and stone the mangoes.*
- *Peel the lime, leaving on as much white pith as possible.*
- *Chop both fruits.*
- *Juice the mangoes, lime and mint leaves, rolling the leaves and putting in between the fruit.*
- *Stir in a dash of rum and mix well. Pour over ice and serve.*

recipes with a twist

juicy variations

- Smoothies

- Uses For Juices

smoothies

All recipes serve one unless otherwise stated.

Smoothies are thicker, more substantial drinks than juices. Bananas or fresh natural yogurt can be used to thicken fruits that may be a little watery, but as with juices you can experiment with all the different fruits and vegetables available. Nuts and seeds can also be a great addition to smoothies, giving extra omega fats, which are very beneficial to health.

To give smoothies their thicker texture, they are finished in a blender to retain some of the 'bits' that are sieved out by juicers.

cherry ripe

This is best with fresh, juicy cherries in season – don't try it until they are really ripe and bursting with flavour.

2 large handfuls of cherries
sparkling water
ice

- *Stone the cherries and juice half of them.*
- *Pour the juice into a blender with the remaining stoned cherries and add the sparkling water and ice.*
- *Blend until smooth and drink immediately.*

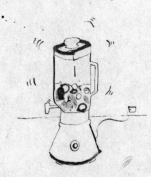

summer smoothie

The best strawberries are the smallest, packed with flavour, that you only find in the summer months.

> 1 peach
> 1 orange
> a few fresh mint leaves
> 2 handfuls of strawberries, tops removed
> 3 tbsp natural yogurt
> ice, to serve (optional)

- *Stone and chop the peach.*
- *Peel the orange, leaving on as much white pith as possible, then chop.*
- *Juice the peach and orange with the mint leaves.*
- *Pour the juice into a blender with the strawberries and yogurt and blend until smooth. Serve poured over ice, or neat.*

juicy variations

raspberry rapple

Raspberries have a distinct flavour so you don't need too many to add a great summery taste. Pick your favourite apples depending on their sweetness and always look for the ripest mango.

4 apples
1 ripe mango
1 handful of raspberries, fresh or frozen

- *Chop the apples and juice two of them.*
- *Peel, stone and chop the mango.*
- *Pour the apple juice into a blender with the mango and remaining 2 apples and blend for 1 minute.*
- *Add the raspberries and blend until smooth. Serve immediately.*

juicy variations

pink slush

This is a delicious drink and so simple with only two ingredients, yet it is bursting with goodness – beta-carotene, vitamin C, vitamin E (from the seeds), and the minerals zinc and selenium.

> **1 handful of strawberries**
> **1/4 large watermelon**

- *Juice the strawberries.*
- *Pour the juice into a blender and add the flesh of the watermelon, including the seeds but not the skin.*
- *Blend until smooth and serve immediately.*

papaya passion

Papayas are full of enzymes that help us to digest complex proteins, such as meat, and they are also believed to be anti-ageing – the perfect excuse for making this delicious smoothie. You need to plan ahead when making this to allow time for freezing some of the ingredients.

1 passion fruit
1 papaya
1 large banana
3 apples
1/2 lime

- *Scoop out the juice from the passion fruits (including the pips) and freeze in an ice-cube tray.*
- *Peel and scoop out the pips from the papaya and cut into chunks, then freeze.*
- *Peel the banana, cut into chunks and freeze.*
- *Chop the apples.*
- *Peel the lime, leaving on as much white pith as possible.*

juicy variations

- *Juice the apples and lime and pour the juice into a blender.*
- *Put the ice-cubes, frozen papaya and banana into the blender and process until smooth. Serve immediately.*

sunset smoothie

This is a real fruity number! You could add a dash of tequila to make it a sunrise, but if you're just going for the healthy option, it is equally great without.

> **2 blood oranges**
> **1/2 medium pineapple**
> **ice**

- *Peel the oranges, leaving as much white pith as possible, and chop.*
- *Juice the oranges.*
- *Peel the pineapple and put in a blender with the ice, then process until smooth.*
- *Pour the orange juice into a glass and top up with the thick pineapple juice. Drink as it is or mix well first.*

uses for juices

Freshly made juices aren't just for drinking. Extend your repertoire by incorporating them into sweet and savoury recipes, using as breakfast or ice-cream toppings and even converting into fresh jellies, ice creams or sorbets.

breakfast

• soaking muesli before eating helps break down the foods for easier digestion and using apple juice rather than milk will help this process further, plus it tastes delicious!

adding flavour

• if you have an abundance of fresh ginger, juice it and store in ice-cube trays in your freezer. When you are making a curry or want to spice up a winter soup, drop in a cube or two of ginger juice.

- spice up the skin of your roast chicken by pouring over ginger juice before roasting, basting from time to time with the pan juices, then use for spicy gravy.

desserts

- stir mango or peach juice into a freshly made fruit salad to give a rich creamy texture.

- use thick fruit juice as a sauce to pour over ice-cream desserts.

marinades

- to tenderise meat, try marinating it in pineapple juice – this juice contains a natural enzyme called bromelain, which breaks down protein.

- orange juice has a great flavour for marinating chicken or fish, or even chopped fruits or vegetables, to be threaded on to skewers and cooked on the barbecue.

juicy variations

fruity yogurts

- all thick fruit juices, such as cherry, mango, peach, nectarine and blueberry, can be stirred into natural yogurt without the need for additional sweeteners – an ideal way to help children to eat their five a day.

fruit juice lollies

- if you have an abundance of fruits (or a children's party coming up) juice your favourite fruits and pour them into ice-lolly containers, place a lolly stick in each one and freeze. If you don't have an ice-lolly container try using an ice-cube tray instead.

fresh fruit jellies

- make your own healthy, nutritious and very tasty jellies using pectin and sugar to sweeten and make them set.

sorbets

- using fruit or vegetables, or even herbs and spices, sorbets are a great way to cleanse the palate between courses or for a slimming but healthy dessert. Heat your fruit juice with some sugar until the sugar has dissolved. Leave to cool. Blend some frozen fruits in a blender with the sweet fruit juice then freeze, stirring from time to time with a fork, until frozen.

coconut milk

- as well as being absolutely delicious to drink, coconut milk has lots of uses in cooking too, especially in Thai recipes. Add to Red Thai curry, sticky coconut rice (normally served with fresh mango slices) or lentil dhals.

juicy variations

step-by-step troubleshooting

- Frequently Asked Questions

- Troubleshooting Guide

frequently asked questions

How do I decide which machine is right for me?

There is so much choice that you need to have a very clear idea of your budget, space and expectations before you start looking. See page 15 which explains the difference between the main machines available, and then decide:

How often do you want to juice?

What are you going to juice?

How much space do you have in your kitchen?

How much do you want to spend?

Research the machines available and ask for personal recommendations.

What is the best way to clean my machine?

Be organised. If you leave your machine for even a few minutes after you have used it, the pulp will start to dry out and stick to the machine, making it far more difficult to clean. Have a bowl of hot, soapy water ready to soak the main parts of the juicer immediately after use. See page 23 for details about the best way of cleaning.

Can I use a blender to make juice?

A juicer works by extracting the juice from a fruit or vegetable, leaving the fibrous part in the pulp that is thrown away. With a blender the whole fruit or vegetable is blended together, leaving the fibre in the juice and producing a thicker, textured drink, known as a smoothie. The juice takes longer for the body to digest and the nutrients aren't as readily available. However, blenders are a great addition to the juicing concept – and are ideal in combination with a juicer to transform juice into smoothies with added ingredients. See Smoothies, page 125.

Do I need a separate citrus juicer?

If your juicer does not come with a dedicated citrus juicer you can juice citrus fruits by peeling and chopping them and feeding them into your normal juicer. This would normally give you more juice and if you are keeping on the pith of the fruit then probably more nutrients too. You can buy dedicated citrus juicers, both manual or electric, but having two machines will take up even more space in your kitchen and mean twice the amount of washing up!

What is the difference between a juice and a smoothie?

A juice is purely that – the juice of the fruit, with none of the fibrous bits. A smoothie contains everything – whole fruits can be used, as can yogurt, milk or nuts. A smoothie is much thicker and sometimes can be more of a meal than a drink! To get the best of both, juice some fruits and put them in your smoothie.

Are all juices suitable for giving to children?

As with all sugar-containing foods and drinks it is best to limit the amount given to children. Smoothies are probably better as you can add milk or yogurt for a good intake of protein to slow down the absorbtion of sugar. Giving your child a fresh juice or smoothie is definitely preferable to giving them a can of fizzy drink, which is full of sugar and contains none of the nutrients that are essential for good health.

Do I have to juice the ingredients in a certain order?

Not generally, but if you are juicing leaves like parsley, spinach, watercress or lettuce (or any other light, loose leaves) it may help if you pack them tightly in between the pieces of a fruit like apples, to ensure they are really compressed and will yield the most juice.

Should I drink certain juices at certain times?

Any time of day is a good time for a juice, and some juices have particular health benefits that alleviate symptoms, or give you an energy boost (see Recipes for Health, page 66). However, you should be aware that juice contains a high concentration of natural sugar, especially those containing exotic fruits, and even some vegetables contain high amounts, and there may be times of the day, such as first thing in the morning, when a high-sugar drink may cause your blood sugar to rise quickly and affect your appetite. Try to balance juices as part of your overall diet.

Can I make my juice in the morning and drink it later in the day?

All juices are best drunk immediately they are made. As soon as you have broken down all the fibres in the juicer, the enzymes in the fruit or vegetable will start breaking down the nutrients, so the longer you leave it the fewer nutrients you will get. However, it is possible to preserve the goodness for a few hours: see page 69 for tips on storing and transporting fresh juice.

Can I add dried fruits to juices or smoothies?

Dried fruits are great to add into smoothies but do be aware that they are very high in sugar – soaking them in water for an hour first will reduce the sugar a little.

When I juice wheatgrass I get a lot of foam – how can I avoid this?

Dunking the wheatgrass in water may help reduce the foam, or try juicing a carrot or stick of celery after the wheatgrass.

troubleshooting guide

I always seem to get a lot of froth in my juice.

Some centrifugal juicers produce juice with froth due to the high speeds at which they work, which incorporates air into the juice. Try using a strainer to strain the juice as it comes out of the machine.

My juice starts to turn brown before I can drink it.

Fruits start to oxidise pretty quickly (think of a cut apple and how quickly it turns brown) and when they are broken down into a juice the process will be even more rapid. Drink your juice the minute you have made it for the best flavour, nutrients and general all-round goodness!

My juice is very thick.

Some fruits like peaches, apricots and mango give very thick juice so it's best to balance them with watery fruits like melon, apples or carrots.

My juice is very watery.

Try to balance your ingredients so you get a juice that tastes substantial. Lots of very watery fruits such as apples and melon will give you a thinner juice than if you added mango, peaches or nectarines.

My juice tastes of the previous recipe.

Thoroughly washing your machine is very important to prevent this happening – see page 23 for cleaning tips. If you are juicing garlic always put it though the machine first to enable the other fruit and vegetables to help clean the machine as they go through.

I don't get very much juice.

Some machines give more juice than others (see pages 17, 18). Always make sure your fruit and vegetables are as fresh as possible, ensuring the maximum yield of juice.

The juice leaks out of my juicer.

This probably means you have not emptied the drum with the pulp in it and the juice is overflowing.

OTHER TITLES AVAILABLE FROM EBURY PRESS:

Tips for Your Breadmaker
9780091909123

Tips for Your Ice Cream Maker
9780091927226

Tips for Your Barbecue
9780091927202

**Available from all good bookshops
or you can order direct from
www.rbooks.co.uk
or 01206 256000**